TRUMPET STARS

SET 1

BY H.A. VANDERCOOK

A COLLECTION OF TRUMPET SOLOS WITH PIANO ACCOMPANIMENT

CONTENTS

RUBANK®

HAL•LEONARD® CORPORATION

7777 W. BLUEMOUND RD. P.O. BOX 13819 MILWAUKEE, WI 53213

Copyright © 2002 by HAL LEONARD CORPORATION
International Copyright Secured   All Rights Reserved

For all works contained herein:
Unauthorized copying, arranging, adapting, recording or public performance is an infringement of copyright.
Infringers are liable under the law.

Visit Hal Leonard Online at
www.halleonard.com

Written by H.A Vandercook, *Trumpet Stars, Sets 1 & 2*, have combined some of Rubank's most popular solos into two collections. After years of remaining the favorite trumpet repertoire pieces of students and teachers, these new book/CD packages provide a unique approach to a better understanding and enjoyment of the music. Tracks 1-6 offers a full performance for trumpet and piano, while Tracks 7-12 has piano accompaniment only. Whether for practice or for listening enjoyment, these book/CD editions will be superb additions to any trumpet music collection.

LYRA
Progressive Etudes for Cornet or Trumpet

Copyright Renewed

Copyright MCMXXXVIII by Rubank Inc., Chicago, Ill.
International Copyright Secured

Lyra

Lyra

VEGA
Progressive Etudes for Cornet or Trumpet

Copyright Renewed

Copyright MCMXXXVIII by Rubank Inc., Chicago, Ill.
International Copyright Secured

Vega

CYGNUS
Progressive Etudes for Cornet or Trumpet

Copyright Renewed

Copyright MCMXXXVIII by Rubank Inc., Chicago, III.
International Copyright Secured

TRUMPET ★ STARS

SET 1

BY H.A. VANDERCOOK

A COLLECTION OF TRUMPET SOLOS WITH PIANO ACCOMPANIMENT

CONTENTS

HAL • LEONARD®
CORPORATION

7777 W. BLUEMOUND RD. P.O. BOX 13819 MILWAUKEE, WI 53213

Copyright © 2002 by HAL LEONARD CORPORATION
International Copyright Secured   All Rights Reserved

For all works contained herein:
Unauthorized copying, arranging, adapting, recording or public performance is an infringement of copyright.
Infringers are liable under the law.

Visit Hal Leonard Online at
www.halleonard.com

LYRA
Progressive Etudes for Cornet or Trumpet

Copyright Renewed

Copyright MCMXXXVIII by Rubank Inc., Chicago, Ill.
International Copyright Secured

VEGA
Progressive Etudes for Cornet or Trumpet

Copyright Renewed

Copyright MCMXXXVIII by Rubank Inc., Chicago, Ill.
International Copyright Secured

CYGNUS
Progressive Etudes for Cornet or Trumpet

Copyright Renewed

Copyright MCMXXXVIII by Rubank Inc., Chicago, Ill.
International Copyright Secured

ANTARES
Progressive Etudes for Cornet or Trumpet

Copyright Renewed

Copyright MCMXXXVIII by Rubank Inc. Chicago, Ill.
International Copyright Secured

ALTAIR
Progressive Etudes for Cornet or Trumpet

Copyright Renewed

Copyright MCMXXXVIII by Rubank Inc., Chicago, Ill.
International Copyright Secured

ARCTURUS
Progressive Etudes for Cornet or Trumpet

Copyright Renewed

Copyright MCMXXXVIII by Rubank Inc. Chicago, Ill.
International Copyright Secured

TRIO

Arcturus

13

Cygnus

14

ANTARES
Progressive Etudes for Cornet or Trumpet

Copyright Renewed

Copyright MCMXXXVIII by Rubank Inc. Chicago, Ill.
International Copyright Secured

Antares

ALTAIR
Progressive Etudes for Cornet or Trumpet

Copyright Renewed

Copyright MCMXXXVIII by Rubank Inc., Chicago, Ill.
International Copyright Secured

Altair

Altair

ARCTURUS
Progressive Etudes for Cornet or Trumpet

Copyright Renewed

Copyright MCMXXXVIII by Rubank Inc. Chicago, Ill.
International Copyright Secured

Arcturus

Arcturus

Arcturus